2016 How Donald Trump Saved America

Jarrad Shelton

2016: How Donald Trump Saved America by Jarrad Shelton
Published by Lulu Press
3101 Hillsborough Street
Raleigh, NC 27607

http://www.lulu.com/

© 2020 Jarrad Shelton.
ISBN 978-1-67811-085-7

Cover by JD Griffin.

2016: How Donald Trump Saved America

Jarrad Shelton

I wrote this book for the coal miner in West Virginia who has watched countless politicians say they care about you, yet sign legislation that puts you out of work.

I wrote this book for the auto worker in Michigan who has watched your leaders sign trade deals that ship your jobs overseas, then smile and say they care about you.

I wrote this book for the farmer in Iowa who has worked 12 hour days for the last 10 years only to see your cost go up and your crop prices go down because our leaders seem to care more about making China happy than they do about protecting American citizens.

I wrote this book for the shop owner on Main Street, America who is barely holding on to a business because that's all you have known all your life as you watch politicians make sweetheart deals for big business who don't need the help.

This is your country too. You deserve the right to Life, Liberty and the Pursuit of Happiness.

Contents

Forward

In September of 2016, I stated that if Hillary Clinton won, America would never see another Republican President elected. I went on to say if Donald Trump won we would never see another Democrat win the White House. The purpose of this book is to explain my reasoning for this. As you read this book, you will see who the party is that cares about America and most importantly, you will see just who it is who cares about you. I give you countless examples of why the Democrats will never win another presidential election.

Enjoy!

Chapter 1

His Big Announcement

June 6, 2015

The sky is clear and the sun is shining bright over

725 5th Ave, New York; where Trump Tower has stood since 1979. Inside was a different story, a hurricane is forming. That hurricane is named Donald John Trump. Trump is preparing to announce his candidacy for the highest office in the world, The Presidency of the United States of America. Thousands of onlookers wait patiently and then he appears. Riding down his golden elevator, he waves to his supporters as they salute their future leader. The media is in full force as they often are anytime "The Donald", as he is often referred to, speaks. Yes, the media loves to hate Donald Trump and this day would be no different.

Mr. Trump settles comfortably on stage surrounded by American Flags. A few last second flashes from the cameras, as Ivanka Trump introduces her father and at 9:01 a.m., Donald Trump begins speaking. He begins by making his case for becoming president. His message is simple-Make America Great Again. In his eyes, and the eyes of many, America has been going downhill for many years. He wants to fix things. After all, he was a builder so who better to fix a broken country, than a builder? Mr. Trump watched America continually lose in many ways, things we should be winning. According to him, we were losing on trade, immigration, and militarily. He had witnessed for decades, many politicians over promise and under deliver. And in some cases, would outright lie to us just to get a vote. Mr. Trump saw many politicians as "weak" leaders and believed America needed a strong man in the highest office of the land. He believed he could be the strong leader who would Make America Great Again.

At first, many people took this announcement lightly. Many people thought this was a publicity stunt. Many people, including myself, thought he would drop out of the race after a few weeks. After all, this was not the first time Donald Trump toyed with the idea of running for president. But something was different this time, a lesson I learned early on. Fortunately, for the other 16 Republican candidates, the media, and entire Democratic Party; it was a lesson learned, much too late.

Chapter 2

Republican Primaries

The Republican Primary in 2016 was the largest and most diverse field for a presidential race ever, totaling 17 declared candidates. That number was surpassed in the 2020 Democratic Primary with to date, 24 declared candidates. Diversity is something the Democratic candidates would struggle with however. Funny how the party who lectures America about inclusion and diversity, ends up with nearly and all-white field of candidates.

Donald Trump was a longshot to win the nomination, let alone the presidency. The field was stacked with many well-known, well respected candidates. Former governors, current governors, former senators, current senators, a son and brother of a previous president, and a brain surgeon, all made up the cast who were running for President of the United States of America. How could a man with no political experience beat that field? Simple, he was going to Make America Great Again.

Prior to the primaries starting, it looked as if former Governor of Florida, son of President George H. W. Bush, brother of President George W. Bush, Jeb Bush, would win the nomination. He had the name recognition, he was a former governor of the "must win" state of Florida, and he had the money, the donors, and the origination. It seemed as if he had everything going his way. Just one problem, he wanted to keep the status quo as if everything was working ok. But Americans knew better. They did not want to keep everything the same. They wanted to Make America Great Again, and Donald J. Trump promised to do so.

The field could be divided into four groups. The grassroots conservatives led by Ted Cruz. The Christian right led by Mike Huckabee and Rick Santorum. The moderates like Jeb Bush, Chris Christie, and John Kasich. Finally, the outsiders like Donald Trump and Ben Carson. Ironically, in a party labeled "racist" by the media, had the most diverse field of candidates ever: two Latinos- Cruz and Rubio, a woman- Carly Fiorina, an Indian American- Bobby Jindal, an African American- Ben Carson, and 5 were children of immigrants.

As the primaries marched on, the field dwindled. It was becoming clear four candidates were in the lead. Florida Senator Marco Rubio, Texas Senator Ted Cruz, Governor John Kasich and businessman Donald Trump. Despite having no political experience Donald Trump was taking the lead. His brash and unapologetic speaking style was the catalyst for his surge in the polls. Trump had no time for political correctness and felt like being politically correct hurt our nation. He was earning the support of blue-collar workers, a group long forgotten by the Democratic Party, as I explain later. Voters with no college education were attracted to

Donald Trump. They felt like he was speaking for them. He was the voice they wanted to hear. To this voting bloc, he spoke of things they wanted to say, but couldn't because the media and people of power rebuked them any time they spoke up. He stood up for them and they loved him for it. The people forgotten by the "elites" in Washington finally had someone speaking up for them. How is it that a billionaire businessman from New York City is able to connect with a coal miner from Kentucky? Simple- he wants to Make America Great Again.

Donald Trump would lead in most polls heading into the first in the nation Iowa caucuses. Ted Cruz would win Iowa, thanks to the support of the grassroots conservatives.

Donald Trump would regain momentum as he won New Hampshire, South Carolina, and Nevada. Super Tuesday would add to his lead, winning 7 of the 11 states. I'm proud to say my home state of Arkansas was won by Donald Trump on Super Tuesday. I had the honor of voting for Donald Trump the Tuesday afternoon of March 1st.

Trump expanded his lead on March 15th, winning 5 of the 6 states. As spring rolled in, the election was looking like there would not be a clear winner. Trump, Cruz, and Kasich were winning enough states to keep the others from winning the nomination. There were whispers of a brokered convention in Cleveland, Ohio.

A brokered convention was the establishment's dream. Trump and Cruz were loathed by the establishment and party leaders. The people who had been in power for a long time truly disliked Cruz and Trump pointing out how weak and ineffective the leaders were.

Given the chance, they would assert their power to keep Ted Cruz or Donald Trump from winning. Once Donald Trump won his home state of New York on April 19th, both Cruz and Kasich were mathematically eliminated from winning the nomination, unless it went to a brokered convention. After Trump won the State of Indiana on May 3rd, Ted Cruz suspended his campaign. This led to Reince Priebus announcing that Donald John Trump would be the 2016 Republican nominee for president. On June 7th, Trump officially broke the number of bound delegates, which eliminated the possibility of a brokered convention. Along the way, Trump broke the record for votes casted, surpassing 14 million. Off to the general election and a former friend and formidable opponent, Hillary Clinton. If you thought the primaries were nasty, wait until you see the bloodbath that awaits in the general election.

Chapter 3

General Election

Unlike the Republican Primaries, the Democratic Primaries were pre-determined. The field was small, mostly because nobody wanted to run; when they knew the outcome. It was no secret that the party leaders at the DNC would ensure that Hillary Clinton would get the nomination. To try and show fairness the DNC allowed a few "token" candidates to challenge Hillary, knowing full well none of them would damage Mrs. Clinton, before the general election. Three no-named, lightweight candidates in Jim Webb, Martin O'Malley, and Lincoln Chaffey alongside admitted Socialist Bernie Sanders rounded out the field beside Mrs. Clinton. It's my personal belief that if the party leaders would have known that a Socialist from Vermont would have gained the traction he did, they would have never let him run.

Hillary would ultimately win the nomination, but would be severely hurt by Bernie Sanders. As a result of Bernie's supporters lobbing jabs at Hillary Clinton, she would limp into the general election where she would face off with former friend, Donald J. Trump.

The 2016 election was the most brutal and bloodiest election ever. The 1828 election between the founder of the Democrat Party, Andrew Jackson and John Quincy Adams, looked like a tea party compared to the 2016 election. What you are about to read is a recap of the 2016 election. An election where the contrast couldn't be clearer. On one side you have a life-long politician who wants to continue the Obama-era policies that hurt many Americans and on the other side a first time politician who wants to Make America Great Again.

Donald Trump ran a populist, America first campaign. He made no secrets that he wanted to put American interest first with every policy he signed off on. On trade, he wanted America to get the best end of the deal. On immigration, he wanted to ensure the immigrants helped America. On every issue he vowed to put America's interest ahead of any other country, any think tank in Washington, even ahead of any donor; something that was unheard of in politics anymore. For this he was hated. He spoke the truth, thus he was attacked. He was not politically correct and said whatever was on his mind. If you were ineffective, he would call you on it. The media hated him for having the courage to tell the truth.

As a result of this, Trump would be labeled by Hillary Clinton and the media as a racist. Likewise his supporters were labeled racist and bigots for supporting him and his America first policies.

Hillary Clinton was running of being the candidate with experience. Having been Secretary of State under President Obama, she saw as a "feather in her cap". But as I will discuss later, it was not a feather in her cap; rather an albatross around her neck. In Mrs. Clinton's eyes Obama had been an effective leader. She embraced many of the Obama era policies and promised to continue them. In fact, she vowed to expand on many of the policies, like Obamacare, that hurt millions of Americans. This book was not meant to degrade Barack Obama, so I will only say this: President Obama was the least business friendly president America has ever had. It was a grave mistake Hillary Clinton made by choosing to run on Obama's economic policies.

Clinton looked like the certain winner and all the polls reflected as much. She was a seasoned politician, a smart lady, and a person with experience. As it turns out, Americans would hold that experience against her.

To understand why Americans held Mrs. Clinton's experience against her, you have to understand the Clintons. For years, corruption seemed to follow both, Bill and Hillary Clinton around. Bill, while the Governor of my home state of Arkansas, had many scandals. None bigger than Whitewater.

Arkansas is full of beautiful land. You don't have to drive very far to find hiking trails, creeks full of fish, mountains for climbing, woods full of many species of animals, ponds for fishing, many lakes full of boaters on any given weekend and rivers for floating and kayaking. We are called The Natural State for a reason.

One of the many rivers is the White River, which flows through Marion County in North Arkansas, not far from Missouri. The river is a haven for anglers. Trout fishing is king on the White River. This attracted investors to set up real estate and cash in on the tourism. A small town named Flippin was a perfect spot for investors. One of the investor in the Whitewater Development Corporation was, then Governor Bill Clinton of Arkansas and wife Hillary along with their associates Jim and Susan McDougal. As it turns out, the business failed. In 1992, when Bill Clinton was running for president, The New York Times published an article that stated then Governor Bill Clinton and wife Hillary Clinton had invested in and lost money in Whitewater Development Corporation.[1] The article got the attention of Laura Jean Lewis, the investigator who was looking into the failure of Little Rock, Arkansas based, Madison Guaranty Savings and Loan Association, also owned by Jim and Susan McDougal.

Lewis began looking at connections between the loan company and the Clintons. On September 2, 1992, Lewis submitted a criminal referral to the FBI, naming Bill and Hillary Clinton as witnesses to the Madison Guaranty case. The case went nowhere as the FBI determined the case lacked evidence. Lewis continued to pursue the case however. She made several more referrals, to no avail. Her continued referrals finally became public knowledge and she was asked to testify before the Senate Whitewater Committee in 1995.

In 1993, David Hale, the source of the criminal allegations against the Clintons, claimed that in November of 1993 Bill Clinton pressured him to provide an illegal $300,000 loan to Susan McDougal, the Clinton's partners in The Whitewater Deal.[2] The allegations were regarded as questionable because it was only after Mr. Hale was indicted in 1993, that he made the allegations against the Clintons.[3]

The U.S. Securities and Exchange Commission investigated. As a result of their investigation the McDougals were convicted for their roles in the Whitewater project. Jim Guy Tucker, Bill

Clinton's successor as governor convicted of fraud in the matter. Susan McDougal spent 18 months in prison for contempt of court for refusing to answer questions related to Whitewater. So everyone involved in the matter, except the Clintons, faced justice.

Bill Clinton was a womanizer and misogynist. He had numerous women accuse him of sexual misconduct, including rape in one instance. One of the accusers was a young intern named Monica Lewinsky. Miss Lewinsky claimed she had performed oral sex on Bill Clinton in the Oval Office of the White House. Now Hillary Clinton, knowing her husband was a womanizer stood by her husband, denying he would do any of it. She went as far as impugning the character of each alleged victim.

Bill Clinton later admitted to having "sexual relations" with Miss Lewinsky. The damage was done to her reputation, however. Americans looked upon this as another time the Clintons got away with something, while others around them were harmed. I will discuss more of these issues later.

Hillary Clinton certainly looked as if she would win big. All the polls indicated Hillary Clinton would win in a landslide and become the first female president and our country's 45th President of the United States. A Republican has a more difficult time winning the Electoral College than a Democrat does. Between California, Illinois, New York, and the other solidly Democrat states on the Northeast; any Democrat has nearly 200 of the 270 needed to win the presidency. So it is easy to see that the path was much easier for Hillary Clinton, than for Donald Trump. A few Rust Belt states won and she would reside at 1600 Pennsylvania for the next 4 years. As you will see later, the Rust Belt would seal Donald Trump's victory.

Donald Trump's path to victory was going to be a challenge, no doubt about it. A challenge he had been working for his entire life. It would be a fight to win, but Donald Trump was a fighter; and had been fighting for what he wanted all his life.

The message was clear- America is screwed up and career politicians have screwed it up. They screwed up on wars, on trade, they screwed up on immigration, and I'm here to fix it. I'm going to Make America Great Again.

From the time Donald won the nomination, television pundits and supposed experts were doubting his chances. They took him lightly, a mistake to say the least. It's true, he could have lost, but to take him lightly and mock him as they did only fueled him and his supporters. A mistake they would soon learn.

Donald Trump certainly came with baggage. Having been in the business world for over 3 decades, and being a rich and powerful man, will often lead to baggage. Being in the public spotlight certainly added to his presidential run, but almost ended his chances of winning before a single vote was cast.

Mr. Trump was a brilliant marketer. He marketed himself as the outsider who could fix things. It was a strategy that drove the media nuts. Donald was the puppet master of the media in the 2016 election. Despite the media hating everything Donald Trump stood for, they could not get enough of him and were there to cover him anytime he spoke. They followed him with cameras throughout the campaign, to Mr. Trump's delight. He understood as long as they were covering him, they kept him relevant and gave him the exposure needed to win a presidential election. While the media was bashing Mr. Trump every day, he would turn to his supporters and say the media is fake and that they were dishonest. This only strengthened his supporters' love for him while strengthening the Medias hate of him. Very few people trusted news outlets like CNN and MSNBC anyway, so when Donald Trump calls them fake, people agree. Donald Trump was manipulating the media who hated him, to in fact help him win the White House.

On the contrary, Mrs. Clinton was very standoffish to the media, doing very few interviews. The few she did participate in were certain friendly outlets. In contrast, Donald Trump would do interviews with anyone who had a press credential. That kind of exposure helped Donald Trump tremendously. In fact, from the beginning of his campaign through February of 2016, Mr. Trump received almost $2 billion in free media; twice the amount Mrs. Clinton received.[4]

Hillary Clinton served as Secretary of State from 2009-2013 under President Barack Obama. As it usually does, controversy followed. Her handling of the Arab Spring, the overthrow of Muammar Gaddafi, and the 2012 embassy attack in Benghazi weighed her down.

The biggest albatross around her neck, was her misuse of her email server. Mrs. Clinton's misuse of her email server was damning in the 2016 election. While Secretary of State, Hillary often traveled to foreign lands, many hostile to the United States. She had access to America's Top Secret information. While traveling abroad she elected to use her own personal email server. She said out of convenience, but many Americans believe she used it because she believed the law did not apply to her. The government goes to great lengths setting up official email accounts that are more secure, but Hillary still chose to use her personal emails. This confirmed to voters that Hillary in fact believed she was above the law.

In July of 2016, then FBI Director, Jim Comey made a rare public announcement. During the press conference, Mr. Comey presented the case of Hillary's misuse of the email server. He presented facts related to the case and claimed that her emails were not as secure as government servers and it was a possibility that her emails could have been hacked into by a hostile nation. He explained that there were in fact classified emails on her server. Mr. Comey went on to say that despite being "careless" with our country's secrets; she would not be charged criminally. This only enraged Americans that the FBI director would make such a strong case against Mrs. Clinton but elect not to recommend charges against her. Another example of Hillary being above the law.

It was also reported that several emails were unable to be recovered from her server, as a result of Hillary and her lawyers erasing emails; even after those emails being subpoenaed. The lawyer even went to length of acid washing the server so nobody could ever see them. Mrs. Clinton stated the erased emails were personal and pertained to daughter Chelsea's wedding. Perhaps, but we will never know thanks to her effort to delete the 30,000 emails in a manner that could never be undone.

Once again, Hillary would not face justice in the eyes of many Americans.

September 9, 2016

Speaking at a LGBT campaign fundraising event in New York City, Hillary made the biggest misstep of her political career. It was one that would turn into an instant meme, T-Shirt slogan and be the talk around America:

> "You know, to just be grossly generalistic, you could put half of Trump's supporters into what I call the basket of deplorables.
>
> Right? They're racist, sexist, homophobic, xenophobic, Islamophobic- you name it."[5]

This is possibly the biggest blunder by a presidential candidate ever. This was just another reason not to like Hillary. Basically, she was saying anyone who does not agree with her ideology, belongs in the "basket of deplorables". Nothing says "vote for me" like degrading half of the country, by calling them names like racist. In my first book "The Intolerant 'Tolerant' Party", I explain just why liberals label people with whom they disagree. This mistake went on for weeks. The very people whom she attacked actually owned it. They began wearing the term "deplorable" as a badge of honor. All this in an effort to stick a thumb in the eye of Mrs. Clinton. It became very clear, Hillary Clinton was not liked by half of America. This was not a recipe for winning a presidential election.

But Donald Trump was not without controversies of his own. In 2004, reality TV was booming. Every network wanted to outdo the other networks by having the highest rated show for the week.

Mark Burnett produced a reality show that tested contestants' business skills in different task every week. They would then be voted off until they found out who had the best business skills. He named his show "The Apprentice". As goes with all reality shows, a host must be found. Who better to host a show about business than a billionaire businessman named Donald Trump? Mr. Burnett pitched the show to NBC and they loved the idea.

The show was a success under Donald Trump, as he drove ratings.

While hosting The Apprentice, Donald Trump made a few cameo appearances on various NBC shows. One of them was the long running daytime soap opera, "Days of our Lives". While on set, Donald gave an interview to Billy Bush of NBC's "Access Hollywood". In the interview Donald Trump made a few lewd comments regarding women. Trump and Bush were bannering back and forth about women and what they do to them. Donald explained to Billy that because he is rich and famous he can do whatever he wanted to a woman and "they don't care". The line that got the most attention was "grab 'em by the pussy". That set off a firestorm. Many people were saying Trump was finished and calling for him to drop out of the race.

Of course the media, who hated Donald Trump anyway, pounced on the opportunity. They had a field day, labeling him sexist and calling him a rapist. Musicians, actors, and other politicians piled on. Most despised him before the comments. Some of the people who piled on had done or said far worse things, but that didn't matter. Donald Trump said these evil things; therefore he must be punished. The mistake seemed as if it would cost Donald

Trump the election, but as stated earlier- Donald Trump is a fighter.

Mr. Trump would not let this ruin chances of saving America. A few days later, he publically apologized, owned his mistake, admitted he made a mistake and moved on. This should serve as a lesson to future politicians, when you make a mistake own it and move on. Don't deflect it and pivot to something else.

Election Day was looming but not before three debates. The first debate was held at Hofstra University on September 26th. Hillary Clinton won the first debate, according to most people. Donald Trump held his own in his first presidential debate. After the debate was over, nothing changed. If you supported Clinton before the debate, you still did. If you liked Trump prior to the debate, you left still supporting him.

The second debate was held at Washington University in St. Louis on October 9th, two days following the Billy Bush tapes. The debate was close but I believe Trump won. I say that because, I believe a small number of votes were changed as a result of this debate. During the debate, Trump stated that if he wins he will appoint a special investigator to look into Hillary's misuse of emails. Keep in mind that a large portion of Americans don't trust Hillary and believe she has used her power to escape justice for years. Hillary, a seasoned lawyer, replies she is thankful people like Donald Trump is not in charge of our legal system. Donald Trump immediately comes back and says what so many Americans were thinking "BECAUSE YOU'D BE IN JAIL". Game over, the crowd goes wild, walk off grand slam, buzzer beater to win the NBA finals, last second Hail Mary to win the Super Bowl, all in one. Donald Trump once again spoke for the forgotten Americans. For the independent voter who didn't really like Donald Trump's antics but didn't trust Hillary and felt she never got what she deserved, to hear someone finally call out Hillary and say she belonged in jail, it felt as if he was speaking for you. It is my belief that was the defining moment of the 2016 election.

The final debate was help at UNLV in Las Vegas on October 19th. The debate was close, probably a tie. But like the first debate, nothing changed.

The stage was set for an election that would change America forever. Would voters want to keep the same old system that worked well for the rich and powerful, or would voters want to Make America Great Again?

Election Day was November 8th. This was an election like none other in my lifetime. I recall the day being exciting. Excitement was in the air. The country was buzzing. All the final polls indicated victory was certain for Hillary Clinton. How would Donald Trump overcome such odds?

Most polls didn't close till late in the evening, so no real data came in until midafternoon. That didn't stop the pundits on TV from declaring Hillary the next president. All morning they were bloviating about how great she is and how America could never elect someone like Donald Trump.

Elections are won by a handful of states. The "swing-states" determine who will be president. States like California, Illinois, and New York will vote for the Democrat and states like Tennessee, Arkansas, and Idaho will vote for the Republican, regardless of who is running. So states like Florida and Ohio decide who sits in the

White House.

For Trump, the path to victory was narrow. He needed to win all the red states and win almost all the swing states. For Hillary, the path is much easier. One swing state like Ohio and off to her victory party.

Things were going as expected once the polls closed on the East Coast. New York, Rhode Island, and the other Northeastern States did what they always do, vote Democrat.

No Republican has ever won the White House without carrying Ohio. That would not change in 2016. Ohio was a must win for Donald Trump. All the campaigning in Ohio paid off as at 9:39 CST, Ohio and its 19 Electoral votes were called for Donald Trump. Donald Trump won Ohio by 8 points, a landslide when you think about it. One hurdle down, but still a long way to go.

The data was coming in from Florida. It seemed like Hillary would pull off a win in Florida, and disrupt Trump's path to victory. Florida's 29 Electoral votes would certainly put Hillary over the top. Not so fast, Florida has 2 time zones and the more conservative panhandle area's votes were not in. Once the 850 area code numbers came in things tightened up. In fact, Donald Trump took the lead. Back and forth for a while until 9:53, when Donald Trump was declared the victor in Florida. Another hurdle down.

Despite having won North Carolina, Florida, and Ohio Mr. Trump was still short of the 270 to win. Still needing to win 2 of the 3 remaining swing states of Wisconsin, Michigan, and Pennsylvania, it still looked like a longshot, but a wider path.

Prior to 2016, Pennsylvania had been a bellwether state for Democrats. Since the votes were so close, it was late before Pennsylvania was called. Would there be enough rural conservative voters in the Western part of the state to offset the metropoles of Pittsburg and Philadelphia? The answer would not come until 12:30 A.M. when Donald Trump was declared the winner, taking all 20 of its Electoral Votes. Another hurdle down. In fact, now it looked like Mr. Trump would soon be President Trump.

While not having the number officially, it certainly looked like Donald Trump would win the White House.

That wouldn't take long. One hour later, Donald Trump was declared the victor in Wisconsin. With Wisconsin's 10 Electoral Votes, President Trump celebrated. How ironic that the state Hillary Clinton failed to campaign in, was the state that sealed a victory for Donald Trump?

Donald Trump is set to become the 45th President of the United States. An accomplishment very few people gave him a chance to do. The victory is the single biggest upset in the history of politics. Harry Truman defeating Thomas Dewey in 1948 did not compare to this.

Chapter 4

Year One

Donald Trump was sworn into office on January 20, 2017 at 12:00 P.M. EST, officially becoming the President of the United States. Time to start Making America Great Again.

Thankfully, the Republicans also won the House of Representatives as well as the Senate in 2016. This made President Trump's first two years much easier. It allowed him to implement his agenda with little resistance from the Democrats.

Undoubtedly, the biggest accomplishment in President Trump's first year was an overhaul of the outdated tax code. The Tax Cuts and Jobs Act passed the House 227-205. No Democrat supported the bill. Think about that for a second. Not one Democrat voted to allow you to keep more of your money. While they claimed to be the party of the "little guy", more often than not, they are for the super wealthy. Democrats are so out of touch with the average voter. The Senate would pass the bill 51-49. Once again, not one Democrat supported lowering your taxes. Democrats are a party of rich people, making laws which benefit rich people.

The Tax Cuts and Jobs Act of 2017 was signed into law by President Trump on December 22, 2017. This was an early Christmas present for the hard-working American citizens. As a result of the bill, Americans saw their taxes go down on January 1, 2020.

For families making less than $250,000.00, thanks to Donald Trump, you would pay 3 or 4% less in taxes depending on your income. Since most Americans made less than $250.000.00 per year, this was a boost in pay to millions of hard-working, American citizens. Keep in mind, every time a paycheck is cashed, that extra $25 dollars per week was a result of policies implemented by Donald Trump and the Republican Party. Also remember that every Democrat in the Congress, objected to Americans keeping more of the money you work for.

Under the new tax law, the standard deduction increased significantly. Going from $12,700 to $24,000 for a family and $6350 to $12,000 for an individual. That would be more money you get back each year when you filed your taxes in April. Even though this was a good thing for the hard-working American citizens, Nancy Pelosi and the other Democrats fought tooth and nail to keep Americans from keeping more of your money.

Another benefit of the new law was the child tax credit. Under the new law, the child tax credit doubled. It went from $1,000 to $2,000 for the first child and $500 for any additional child. No one should oppose giving a single mom, who relies on her income tax return to catch up on bills, or take a trip with her kids, or buy some new clothes for her child, more money. The Democrats did.

Every Democrat, when given the chance to vote for The Tax Cuts and Jobs Act, elected not to do so. Just remember the next time they say they care about the "little guy", they are lying.

The bill also removed the crippling ACA individual mandate. Under the ACA, a person was mandated, by the government, to buy health insurance. Of course, this was unconstitutional as the Federal government cannot compel anybody to purchase something. They argued before the Supreme Court, that they were "taxing" American citizens for not having health care, which is perfectly legal. Either way the mandate made no sense. The government was forcing people to buy something they may not want or may not be able to afford. If they did not buy it, they were punished by paying a tax. Donald Trump could see how insane this policy was. So as part of the Tax Cuts and Jobs Act, the mandate was removed. Of course this was a good thing and millions of Americans celebrated not having to buy something they might not want. To the Democrats, this was terrible. Just another example of how out of touch the Democrats were with the American people.

For many years, American companies were having to compete with foreign companies for business. I believe competition is good, but it must be fair. Under the old law, if a person wanted to open a business and be based in America, you would have to pay a 35% tax rate. That same business owner could move the company to China, India, Mexico, or any other country, and pay a lower tax rate. This rate was much lower. Less taxes equals more profit. This incentivized offshoring, which is why factories all throughout America were empty. That company who used to be in Anytown, USA, where they hired 100 people, making a good wage; is now in Mexico City. This was very unfair to America. Being a businessman, President Trump knew this all too well. Under the new law, Cooperate tax rate went from 35% to 21%. This meant that companies in the US could stay here, and still be competitive in the global market. More American companies meant more jobs for the American citizens. Once again Donald Trump was Making America Great Again. Yet, somehow the Democratic Party was against this.

Any country that has an abundance of oil, is a prosperous nation. America has an untold amounts of oil all throughout our great nation. One of the areas that has a plethora of oil is Alaska. ANWR, Arctic National Wildlife Refuge, had been off limits for any exploration of oil for many years. Along came President Trump and said we should explore this vast area and harvest the oil. This of course angered the Democrats and the environmentalists. Doesn't matter, Donald Trump thought "America first" in everything he did. As a result of President Trump, ANWR began allowing drilling for oil.

One of the most important jobs any president has to do is appoint judges. The 3 co-equal branches of government that our founders set up is a system of checks and balances. The Legislative Branch writes the laws, the Executive Branch enforces the laws written by the Legislative Branch, and the Judicial Branch consist of courts set up to determine if the laws are legal, according to the Constitution. For many decades, the Democratic Party has relied less on public opinion, i.e. voting, and more on corrupt, partisan judges to push through their leftist agenda. No need to win over a majority of the public on a radical idea, like abortion or same sex marriage, when you can just appoint judges who think like you do.

In President Trump's first year in office he appointed more circuit judges than any time in the history of America. He also set records for the first year judicial appointment to the Federal Appeals Court. On December 14th, 2017 President Trump set a record for most Federal Appeals Judges appointed in the first year of a presidency. President Trump believed in the Constitution and vowed to appoint judges who believed in the rule of law, not made laws from the bench as many judges do.

The most public judicial appointment President Trump made was the appointment of Justice Neil Gorsuch to the Supreme Court. The final stop in determining if a law is constitutional is the Supreme Court. Justice Gorsuch was appointed to fill the vacancy left behind by the late Justice Antonin Scalia. Like Justice Scalia, Justice Gorsuch was an originalist who followed the Constitution completely. The fact that Justice Gorsuch interpreted the law as it was written, rather than changing the law to fit his agenda; truly scared Democrats. Mr. Gorsuch was a threat to any lunatic, liberal ideas so he had to be stopped by the Democrats. They opposed this appointment with everything they had, attacking Justice Gorsuch every day.

If you ask Americans, what is the most important thing to them, almost everyone will answer a vibrant economy. The economy has been and always will be the number one factor when voting for a president. If the economy is doing well and if people are feeling good about the economy, any sitting president will get re-elected. The economy overrides any other issue. The resurgence of the American middle-class under President Trump was like no one before him.

Unemployment in 2016, Obama's last year in office, stood at 4.7% overall. Breaking that down further:

Unemployment: 2016	
White	4.3%
Black	8.1%
Asian	3.0%
Hispanic	5.8%

Those are the real numbers taken straight off the Bureau of Labor stats.[6] Compare that to President Trump's first year in office. Overall 2017 unemployment numbers ended at 4.1%. Breaking that down further:

Unemployment: 2017[7]	
White	3.6%
Black	7.3%
Asian	3.0%
Hispanic	4.7%

Nearly a 1% drop for all citizens, yet somehow the Democrats opposed this. This type of opposition was dangerous to our country. Just another example of why American citizens will never elect another Democrat to the White House.

Gross Domestic Product is the rate of growth in a country. Each country in the world judges the strength of its nation by the GDP number. GDP provides the public a snapshot of the economy. A healthy economy means more consumer confidence. Obviously, the higher the GDP, the better state of the economy. Under President Obama, GDP never reached 3% growth. For 8 years, America never saw 3% growth. Never before in the history of our country had a president not achieved 3% growth.

In 2016, Obama's last year, GDP was 1.6%.[8] In 2017, GDP was at 2.7%.[9] So in one year, the American economy grew over 1%. A business-friendly economy was already paying off. The American public was feeling good about the economy and ready to spend money.

One of the biggest obstacles of a growing economy is crushing regulations. More regulations to a business usually means hiring less employees and less investments back into the business. As of December 2017, President Trump policies have resulted in a 22-1 deregulation ratio.[10] Crippling regulations often mean businesses closing or having to reduce the workforce. These regulations more often than not effect small businesses the most. Large companies have the ability to hire the right lobbyist who works out some sweet deal for big business. The small shop owner who hires five employees and barely makes enough to keep the doors open, cannot hire the best lawyers and accountants to look for loopholes. So every time a politician comes up with some senseless regulation, a small business comes closer to closing down. Donald Trump understood that. He knew what would happen when America was faced with numerous regulations. As many economist have stated, President

Trump has been the most pro-business president we have ever had.

President Trump's signature issue he ran on in 2016 was undoubtedly illegal immigration. From his first speech declaring he was running for president, everyone knew where he stood on illegal immigration.

Illegal immigration has been a growing problem for decades. Donald Trump had witnessed our leaders, on both side of the aisle, turn a blind eye to illegal immigration for years. He also saw all the negatives that came with unchecked illegal immigration. He had the courage to tell the truth, and for that he was labeled a racist by his opponents and by the media.

President Trump promised to do something about the growing problem, not just say "we will look into it" as so many leaders before had said. His solution: build a wall. Walls work, always have. There is a reason why ancient cities built walls around their city. That is why we build our houses with walls. Wall keep the people out who don't belong, but has a door to allow people we want in. To most Americans, this made sense. Sure, in the faculty lounge at Harvard, this was racist, but to the factory worker in Green Bay, Wisconsin; it was logical. President Trump wanted to build a wall along the southern border with a "big beautiful door". Democrats hated him for this. This was part of his plan to Make America Great Again, something the Democrat Party was against.

President Trump made promises and he worked to fulfill them. As of December 17, 2019, according to the U.S. Customs and Border Protection's Mark Morgan, 93 miles of new wall have been built. It has been a slow process as President Trump has been resisted by every Democrat, the media, and even some RINO Republicans. The border wall is being built and will continue being built until our entire southern border is protected. In 2017, illegal border crossing arrest hit a 46 year low, and were down 25% from the previous year.[11]

Some might say, why do you need a border and who cares if illegal aliens sneak in our country? Just ask one of the thousands of angel parents who lost someone they love because an immigrant was here illegally and you will see why it matters. Everyone knows the story of Kate Steinle, the young woman walking on a pier in San Francisco, who was shot and killed by an illegal alien that had been deported numerous times only to return. There are literally hundreds of stories like that of Kate that people have never heard; stories like this one. This story comes from a personal dear friend of mine named Sabine Durden. This is truly a story of the American dream. A dream that ended all too tragically. Something that never had to happen.

I live in the small, rural town in the Southwest corner of Arkansas, called Nashville. Yes, there is a Nashville, Arkansas. There is also a Murfreesboro, Arkansas not far from Nashville. If you are familiar with Tennessee, you understand what I am referring to. The town I live in has about 6,000 people living in it. A few miles south of Nashville is an even smaller town called Mineral Springs. That is where the story begins.

One of Mineral Springs' 1,500 residents is Sabine Durden-Coulter, who moved there in 2017. Sabine was born in Germany, but moved to the United States in 1989 using a Resident Alien Card. She brought her son Dominic with her hoping to live the American

Dream. She settled in California, where she became a citizen on February, 23 1996. Life was well with Sabine and Dominic. Nicknamed, German Chocolate, Dominic was employed as a dispatcher with the Riverside Sheriff Department. At age 30, he had aspirations of becoming a helicopter pilot with the Sheriff Department. Sadly, that dream would end on July, 12, 2012.

The morning of July 12th Dominic was riding his motorcycle to work. On his way to work, Dominic was sideswiped by an illegal alien named Juan Zacarias Tzun. Juan has 2 previous DWI convictions, and when tested had alcohol in his system the morning he hit and killed Dominic. He had no driver's license and two prior felonies. One for armed robbery and another for grand theft larceny. Yet, thanks to liberal politicians like those in California, Juan was free and roaming the state. Thanks to poor leaders like the ones in California, Dominic is no longer living.

Juan was charged with misdemeanor vehicular manslaughter without gross negligence. He spent just 35 short days in jail. Got that! Come into our country illegally, get drunk, kill someone, and serve a month in jail. This is bullshit! If you think illegal aliens get treated better than citizens, you would be correct.

Following the short stay in jail, he spent a little over a year in an Immigration Detention Center until he was deported on March 18, 2014. Thanks to California's welcoming of illegal aliens, it is likely Juan is back in California. Sabine says she watches the news every night just anticipating, seeing his face as they talk about another victim he has killed.

Imagine for a moment that you are one of the thousands of angel parents. Angel moms or dads who has lost a son or daughter that you will never see get married, you will never see them get a promotion at work, you will never see them teach their child to throw a baseball; all while the person who killed them gets punished lightly. It is beyond aggravating! Politicians that push these policies should be ashamed of themselves, but they are not. They are not because at the end of the day, illegal immigration is about one thing: VOTES!

Chapter 5

Year Two

2018 rings in with a bang! The economy is rolling, people are spending money, tax cuts are about to kick in, and Americans are feeling good. 2018 is an election year, so House and Senate members who are up for reelection are in full campaign mode, so do not expect much to happen. Not so fast, President Trump has not finished Making America Great Again.

One of the issues voters had to decide on in 2016 was the Supreme Court. Voters understood that the next president would appoint at least one justice, probably two, and possibly three more justices. The Supreme Court determines how the country will be governed. A liberal-leaning court means any liberal law that gets challenged will likely be upheld. Voters spoke in 2016, electing President Trump. Americans made it clear, they do not want a liberal-leaning court.

When Justice Anthony Kennedy announced he would retire, President Trump was tasked with finding a replacement. President

Trump was looking for a young, conservative judge to replace Justice Kennedy. He found a young man named Brett Kavanaugh. Mr. Kavanaugh was certainly qualified, but to the left; that did not matter. Justice Brett Kavanaugh being appointed to the Supreme Court enraged the already unstable left. They hated this man. Their attacks were relentless. The normal attacks came out- racist, sexist, misogynist, the regular rhetoric the left uses when they disagree with someone. The left hated Brett for many things, but most of all was his stance on abortion. To the left, abortion is sacred. Roe v Wade is the most important thing to the Democratic Party. They will do anything to protect this law. Smearing a Supreme Court Justice, for no apparent reason, is not off limits to the left; so long as it serves the greater good of protecting aborting a baby at any time, for any reason. Unfound accusations of rape and wild accusations going back 20 years were not enough of a smear tactic to keep the Senate from confirming Justice Brett Kavanaugh. On October 6, 2018, Justice Brett Kavanaugh was sworn in as a justice on the Supreme Court. With another conservative justice, the court now leaned to the right. Another step to Making America Great Again.

Another signature issue Donald Trump ran on in 2016 was broken trade deals. Donald Trump had watched for years as America lost on every trade deal we made. China was getting the best of America. A growing country, China had aspirations of becoming the world's superpower. President Trump knew he could beat China, so long as he made smart deals that put American interests first. Understanding that China depends on America, far more than we depend on them, President Trump set out to break the Chinese economy with tariffs. A gamble perhaps, but it paid off. Thanks to the tariffs put in place, China lost $35 billion in the first half of

2018. The tariffs also helped get China to the negotiation table for an upcoming big trade agreement.

2018 was a fantastic year for minorities. Black unemployment reached the lowest level ever recorded in 2018. This was a direct result of policies put forth by President Trump. While I will not say the Democrats were against more minorities working, I will say their hatred of Donald Trump far outweigh the idea of more black people working. If you asked a liberal if they could get President Trump out of office, but it meant more minorities being unemployed, most liberals would make that sacrifice. Same thing was true for Latinos. In 2018, unemployment rates fell below 5%. In fact, there had only been 14 months of less than 5% jobless numbers for Latinos and 13 of the 14 months happened under President Trump.[12] If Donald Trump is a racist, as the media says, he is an ineffective racist. Truth is, President Trump is no racist, he only wants what is best for America; something the Democrats hate.

Oil production is, has been, and always will be the pathway to prosperity of any nation. A nation who has an abundance of oil is a wealthy nation. America has a vast supply of oil and President Trump was going to capitalize on that. Thanks to greenlighting the Key Stone Pipeline, fracking, more off-shore drilling, and common sense policies, America became the world's leading oil producer, surpassing Russia and Saudi Arabia.

As 2018 was closing, America faced its mid-term elections. If history repeated itself, Republicans were set to lose seats in the House of Representatives. As it often goes, Republicans lost 41 seats and lost the majority in the House. However, 2018 ended on a high note, the economy was rolling, peace and prosperity was around the corner.

In 2019, Nancy Pelosi would be the speaker of the House so resistance would be ramped up, but no one could see what was about to happen.

Chapter 6

Year Three

A new year was upon us, and things were still going well. Paychecks were up, taxes were down, and all was well on the home front. This, of course, enraged the Democrats even further. If things are going well, the chances of beating President Trump in 2020 goes way down. The Democrats will have to come up with something, but what will it be?

Just like the previous years, wages were up; especially for the lowest 10% earners seeing a 7% wage growth.[13] Jobs are the key to a successful administration and 2019 would see the 16th straight month of 3% job growth.[14]

Good Trade deals are a hallmark of President Trump. NAFTA, signed into law by Bill Clinton in 1992 was a disaster for America. President Trump was ready to replace NAFTA with the USMCA. Even though USMCA would help America, Nancy Pelosi refused to bring it up for a vote until December.

Look for President Trump to sign USMCA sometime in 2020.*

2019 was plagued by impeachment, with Congress putting forth very few things to help America. Despite resistance in 2019, the year ends on a high note. The economy is booming for everyone. More minorities are turning their backs on the Democrats. The "walk-away" campaign is real. Conservatives like Candace Owens, Diamond and Silk, Larry Elders, and Kanye West are exposing the Democratic Party for the frauds they are. The Democrats are scared for their political future.

2020 will be a great year. President Trump will be re-elected. The economy will continue to roar. President Trump will continue Making America Great Again.

* This section was written prior to the USMCA being signed into law on January 29, 2020.

Chapter 7

Rust Belt States

The Rust Belt is a sector of America that is mostly in the Midwest. Part of New York, Pennsylvania, West Virginia, Ohio, Indiana, Michigan, Northern Illinois, Eastern Iowa, and Southern Wisconsin all make up the Rust Belt.

The Rust Belt states have witnessed the decline of their area since 1980. Steel mills being shut down, car manufacturing plants shipped to Mexico, West Virginia coal mines being regulated out of business, all by ineffective leaders.

At one time, thanks to automobile manufacturing, Detroit was one of the richest cities in America, but no longer. As of 2018, Detroit has lost 29.3% of its population.[15] Other towns in Michigan were hit hard as well. Saginaw and Flint, Michigan lost 20% of their population as well. You would think this would be alarming to the Democrats, but any policy Donald Trump put forth to help the great people in the Rust Belt states was met with resistance by the Democratic Party. USMCA would benefit this region, but rather than pass it right away to help the forgotten Americans, Nancy Pelosi and the other Democrats wanted to play political games. Michigan broke for President Trump in 2016. This marked the first time a Republican had won in Michigan since George H.W. Bush in 1988. President Trump's narrow .23% margin in 2016, I believe will be even larger in 2020. The fact that the state was considered a "swing state" in 2016, is a story all in itself. How is it that a state that has voted Democrat for over 20 years, is all of a sudden a "swing state"? The answer is simple- the forgotten Americans were tired of the Democrats ineffectiveness. Thanks to President Trump Making America Great Again, you will never see a Democrat win Michigan again.

Ohio was hit hard as well under NAFTA. Between 1993-2015, Ohio lost 302,000 manufacturing jobs.[16] That would be alarming to someone who cared about its citizens, but Democrats would rather impeach President Trump than work with him to solve a huge problem. Democrats lost Ohio in 2016, by 8.13%. They had not lost Ohio since 2004. It is obvious the voters of the state have had enough of the broken promises and failed policies of the Democratic Party. For many years Ohio has been a "swing state". It is my belief that the policies President Trump is putting forth to strengthen Ohio's job market and thanks to the Democrats being very ineffective, Ohio will no longer be considered a "swing state", but rather a red state.

Economic prosperity was coming back to the Buckeye State. Weekly wages hit an all-time high in the first quarter of 2019, at $1033.[17] Unemployment in Ohio was at 4% in July of 2019. The state gained 4500 jobs according to the Ohio Department of Jobs and Family Services.[18] You would think that Democrats would be happy to know that jobs are coming back to the Midwest, but hatred for President Trump far outweighed any good news for the forgotten men and women.

Pennsylvania has been Steel Country for many years. Steel mills all throughout the Keystone State, provided jobs and economic prosperity to its residents.

NAFTA hit Pennsylvania very hard. Since 1994, Pennsylvania lost over 315,000 manufacturing jobs. 1 in 4 residents lost 20% of their income.[19] Thanks to NAFTA, income inequality rose significantly. Pennsylvania's richest 10% own 46% of the state's income as opposed to 39% before NAFTA.[20]

Like Michigan, Pennsylvania had voted for the Democrats since 1988. Going into the 2016 election, most "experts" viewed Pennsylvania as solidly Clinton. Election Day was another story. President Trump won 56 of the 67 counties in Pennsylvania. Pennsylvania residents were tired of the weak leaders in the Democratic Party and tired of the Democrats overlooking them. Since being elected, President Trump has worked to keep China from dumping cheap steel into America, which is reviving a failing economy.

The notion that a Republican could win in Pennsylvania was unheard of, but Donald Trump did it. He was able to connect with the great people of Pennsylvania and showed them how ineffective Democrats had been. In his first term, President Trump was keeping his promises and Making America Great Again. Because of this it is my belief that Pennsylvania will never vote for a Democrat again.

Like many other states, NAFTA hit Wisconsin hard. From 1994-2019, Wisconsin lost 46,647 jobs or 9.1%.[21] The Economic Policy Institute found by 2010, 14,500 jobs had been lost or displaced in Wisconsin due to the trade deficit with Mexico, under NAFTA.[22] The Economic Policy Institute also found that 68,600 jobs had been lost or displaced in Wisconsin since China joined the World Trade Organization in 2001.[23]

In 2016, Donald Trump was projected to lose big in Wisconsin. The state had not voted for a Republican since 1984 when they voted for Ronald Reagan. Since Hillary believed Wisconsin was a safe state she neglected to visit the state any time during the election. That would prove to be a grave mistake. Donald Trump narrowly won the Badger State, officially making him president. Donald Trump made promises to the state and they gave him a chance by electing him. Wisconsin, like many other Rust Belt states were tired of weak leaders who promised everything while delivering nothing. Thanks to the booming economy, NAFTA being replaced, and a leader who actually cared about the voters; Wisconsin will forever be a Red State.

Chapter 8

Forgotten Americans

The "forgotten Americans" is a class of people who are looked over, looked down upon, passed off as ignorant rubes, seen as simple minded, and of no importance to the "elites" of this great nation. The forgotten Americans live in all 50 states and are of all race and creeds. They want a simple life and want to be respected for who they are.

The forgotten American is the truck driver who gets up before the sun rises so he can make the 600 mile roundtrip run all in one day so he can eat dinner with his wife and kids. The forgotten American is the plumber who gets up in the middle of the night because someone has a toilet that is flooding the house. The forgotten American is the waitress who supports two kids by taking every extra shift she can, all while teaching her kids the basics of life.

The forgotten American is wheat farmer in Topeka, Kansas who works 12 hour days, 7 days a week only to see weak leaders sign trade deals that ultimately cut the price of crops in half while the cost of fuel doubles. The forgotten American is the department store owner in Brunswick, Georgia who makes very little profit each year, but watches corrupt leaders sign legislation that give tax breaks to companies who make billions of dollars profit each year. The forgotten American is the factory worker in Omaha, Nebraska who prays each night that he still has a job the next day, because for years ineffective leaders write laws that make it profitable to ship your job overseas.

The forgotten American is the gas station clerk who fears for her life every night because crime is on the rise thanks to weak leaders who prioritize criminals over law abiding citizens. The forgotten American is the police officer who leaves the house every morning not knowing if that's the last time he will kiss his wife and kids goodbye, all because cowardly leaders take the side of criminals and vilify the people who protect law and order. The forgotten American is the firefighter who in the face of danger runs in the burning building to save complete strangers, but can't save his own family from the already high taxes that corrupt leaders continue to raise.

Truth is the forgotten Americans are the millions of hard working Americans who voted for Donald Trump in 2016. We respect law and order and are not ashamed of it. We love our guns and have no time to be lectured by some celebrity who has 10 armed guards with them at all times. We love our SUV and refuse to listen to some liberal politician who flies private jets everywhere tell us we are destroying the planet because our car only get 15 miles per gallon. We love red meat and will not let a tofu eating hipster tell us we are destroying America because we like to eat meat.

We will not be silenced. We love God and we respect our neighbors.

Chapter 9

Trade Deals

As mentioned earlier, NAFTA cost Americans thousands of jobs. Signed into law by Bill Clinton, NAFTA began January 1, 1994. NAFTA resulted in 20 years of stagnant wages for American citizens. The horrible trade deals cost 700,000 jobs lost. Most from California, Texas, Michigan, and other manufacturing states.[24]

NAFTA also strengthened U.S. companies' abilities to force workers to accept lower wage and benefits. Company managers could tell their workers that they intended to move to Mexico unless the workers lowered the cost of labor. In some instances, companies would load machinery and say they were headed to Mexico.[25]

NAFTA was a topic in the 1992 Presidential Debate. Listen to Ross Perot in the debate:

"We have got to stop sending jobs overseas. It's pretty simple: if you're paying $12, $13, $14 an hour for a factory workers and you can move your factory south of the border, pay a dollar an hour for labor, have no health care that's the most expensive single element in making a car- have no environmental controls, no pollution controls, and you don't care about anything but making money, there will be a giant sucking sound going south.

When [Mexico's] jobs come up from a dollar an hour to six dollars an hour, and ours go down to six dollars an hour, and then it's level again. But, in the meantime, you've wrecked the country with these kinds of deals."[26]

Ross Perot was absolutely correct. As a result of NAFTA, companies laid off thousands of workers, went to Mexico, paid the new workers 1/10 of the American wages, had no healthcare expenses, and the CEO of the company would reap the benefits, often walking away with millions of dollars in bonuses. Then if not bad enough, the company would turn around and ship the products made in Mexico back to the United States and sell them to the very people they just laid off. The system was rigged for the ultra-wealthy.

So along comes President Trump and points out how corrupt the system was and says we need to replace NAFTA with a more

American friendly deal. This, of course outraged the Democrats. While they want to claim they are for the working class and say that raising the middle class up is very important to them, their actions say otherwise. Every time President Trump proposes something to help the poor and middle class, Democrats protest and storm the streets; usually demanding his removal from office.

There is a bright light here though. Donald Trump signed the United States Mexico Canada Agreement (USMCA) at the G-20 summit in Buenos Aires on 11-30-2018. USMCA will replace the outdated, unwise NAFTA. Unlike NAFTA, under the USMCA, companies cannot up and move to Mexico as easily, nor is it as lucrative.

Under NAFTA, any automobile sold in America, had to have at least 62.5% of that automobile, made in America. Under USMCA that number moves to 75%. In another words, if you buy a car at your local car lot, 75% of that car purchased will be made in America. That is many more jobs created in America. That is thousands more people hired in Detroit to assemble the car. That is thousands more people hired at Cooper Tire in Texarkana, Arkansas, making more tires to go on the car. That is thousands more people hired at Johnson Controls in Glendale, Wisconsin, making batteries for General Motors cars. It means thousands of more workers hired all across America, reviving an industry that been slumping for years.

USMCA makes moving a company to Mexico for cheap labor nearly impossible. In the agreement 45% of any automobile manufactured in North America, must be made in a factory that pays a minimum of $16 per hour. So if you work at a Ford Factory in Detroit, Michigan making $20 per hour, you don't have to fear your job being shipped to Mexico where they can pay the employees $4 per hour. That is job security that everyone wants. No employee should have to fear their job being outsourced because our leaders make weak deals that allow companies to move with no repercussion.

USMCA would certainly help the blue collar worker, but rather than bring it up for a vote, Nancy Pelosi held up the vote because she did not want to give President Trump a victory.* Just remember the next time Democrats ask for your vote and tell you that they care about you, they don't. They are lying to you. They care about one thing and that's power.

Chapter 10

Border Security

The classic saying by the "open border" crowd is: "America was founded by immigrants". While that is true, at the time of our country's founding, America was a totally different place. At the time of our founding, we were a large country in terms of land mass compared to the number of people living here. We needed to fill the vast lands up with people to grow a country.

Fast-forward to 2020 and things are much different. America has around 330 million people living in it. Land is scarce, cities are overcrowded, homes can't be built fast enough, and allowing millions of people to flood an already overcrowded country makes no sense. Drugs pour into our country every day across the southern border, so the idea that we do not need a barrier to slow immigrants down and slow the drug trade down is completely asinine.

Illegal immigration has been a real problem in America for decades. Illegal immigration spiked in the 1980's thanks to the growing economy under Ronald Reagan. Reagan tried to do something about the problem, by offering a onetime amnesty for the people already here, in exchange for border security. The Democrats reneged on the promise, of course and the problem has been expanding ever since. The best estimate is we have about 12 million illegal aliens in America. The truth is, nobody knows what the true number is and nobody ever will. It is impossible to know and that is not only foolish for a country to not know who is here, it is dangerous. Why is it ok for the government to know everything about its natural born citizens but it knows nothing about the people who sneak in here in the dark of night?

With an open border, as most Democrats call for; people can come and go as they please. With no restraints, an illegal alien can come into America as he want, work a while, maybe commit crimes, and go back to Mexico and never face justice. Most are probably good people who want to better their family and escape the poverty that is in Mexico. But like Sabine Durden, we have a legal channel to come to America. America is the most generous country on the planet, allowing thousands of people from foreign countries the opportunity to come here and work and possibly become a citizen. All we ask is do it the right way.

Just as there are honest, hardworking, immigrants who come to America, there are criminals who come to America with the only intentions of a life of crime. Some bring drugs into this country, some come here and kill Americans, some come and rape Americans, and it is a system that cannot go on in a civilized country. Most sincerely want a better life, but to allow anyone to come here with no restrictions is asking for bad things to happen.

One of the consequences of illegal immigration is the effect it has on wages. Wages for Americans, in the low skilled labor sector are driven down as a result of illegal immigration. For example- if a farmer needs to hire 20 people to maintain his farm, and he has 20 legal citizens who must pay taxes and requires $12 per hour to work the farm come and apply, and then has 20 illegal aliens who don't have to pay taxes so they can work for $10 per hour, who do you think the farmer will hire? It is completely logical to say that this system does not benefit the American citizen. But if you dare speak up, you are labeled a racist by the elites in Washington. President Trump had the courage to say it and point out the injustice that goes along with illegal immigration.

Possibly the most important reason to build a wall along the southern border is to slow the massive drug trade that is happening. Drugs like cocaine, meth, and opioids flow into America with little obstruction. Thousands of American citizens die each year from the poison Mexican cartels ship to America. Everyone who reads this book will have their own story of someone whose life was ruined by drugs. Small towns all throughout America are disappearing thanks to opioids. The border wall proposed by Donald Trump would slow down the drug trade, exponentially. It would not stop the drugs from coming to America all together, because as long as America has a thirst for drugs, someone will fill it. But the first step is building the wall to slow the trade down.

A wall would save the mom in Sandpoint, Idaho from watching her daughter full of life and full of dreams die from overdosing on heroin. A border wall would save the star quarterback, who has dreams of one day playing in the NFL from getting hooked on meth his senior year of high school. Only to drop out of college his freshman year and spend a lifetime of in and out of jail. Yes, a border wall would help America, so of course; Democrats oppose it. Democrats oppose it because a border wall means stopping an entire future voting class from coming to America. And because illegal immigrants were the key to Democrats being in power forever, ILLEGAL IMMIGRANTS MUST BE PROTECTED AT ALL COST. Who cares if a few American citizens die as a result of the plan? They are collateral damage, so who cares. Donald John Trump cares and that's why he wants the wall to be built.

For decades, African Americans have almost entirely voted for Democrats; going back to Lyndon B. Johnson signing The Great Society Law on April 11, 1965. I explain why he signed the law in my previous book, "The Intolerant 'Tolerant' Party". The Democrat Party relies heavily on the African American voting bloc, really taking them for granted when you think about it. Democrat politicians show up in an election year, promise to do this, or fix that, help you here; only to get elected, spend the next few years in Washington, lining their own pockets with millions of dollars, while the very people who voted for them suffer. This has gone on for years. The pattern is repeated every 2, 4, or 6 years.

Black poverty has declined over the years, but not at the rate of other races. It is still above the median poverty line. There are many factors to why this is the case, but Democratic policies put forth have certainly contributed. Here's one example- Facts show that students do far better academically in charter schools. So given that, you would think everyone would embrace "school choice" which would allow students born in a poor neighborhood that is served by a failing public school system, to go to a charter school of their parents' choice. The Democrats object to this vehemently. They oppose school choice because they are in cahoots with the powerful teachers union who, if given the chance would put every charter school out of business. Kids having a chance at success is irrelevant. Money and power mean more to the Democrats than children having a chance at a decent education.

So along came Donald Trump and he pointed out the failings and ask for the votes of African Americans. He exposed the Democrats and all their failings. Slowly the African American community has been leaving the Democrat Party. People like Diamond and Silk, Candace Owens, Larry Elder, and Kanye West are vocal allies of Donald Trump who expose the Democrats for the frauds they are.

The fact that your most reliable voting bloc was leaving might be alarming to a party, but the Democrats had a plan. The plan was to import millions of new votes in the way of illegal aliens and replace the black voters. They wanted an open border because it meant that they would have an always reliable voting class for decades. Donald Trump's proposed wall was an obstruction to their plan and therefore they must oppose it.

Chapter 11

Impeachment

Donald Trump won the presidential election on November 8, 2016. He was sworn into office on January 20, 2017 at 12:00 EST. Prior to being sworn into office, before he signed any law, before he made any executive order, prior to him doing him doing one thing to hurt or to help America, there were some in the media and in Congress calling for his impeachment. I want you to think about that for a minute. Before Donald Trump could be called President Trump, members of Congress wanted him to be removed from office. They didn't care what the people wanted. To them, Donald Trump was a threat. He was a threat because he challenged their power, and to Democrats: power is everything. Once President Trump was sworn into office and started fulfilling his promises, which was taking power away from many Democrats, the calls for impeachment became louder and included more people.

In December of 2017, Al Green, a Democrat from Texas, officially filed a motion to impeach Donald Trump. The reason for impeachment was irrelevant. "President Trump is bad, and must be removed" was enough for Al Green to file the bogus articles. Republicans controlled the House and the articles failed. This would be a foreshadowing of things to come once the Democrats regain the House. The fact that the articles of impeachment failed big was not going to stop Democrats. They had a plan. Their plan was to blame an old foe.

When you think of the Cold War you might think of Ronald Reagan, USSR, or Mikhail Gorbachev. You might even think of Rocky Balboa defeating Ivan Drago in Moscow on Christmas Day. Whatever jogs your memory of the Cold War is wrong, according to the Democrats. Democrats said the Cold War was alive and well and Russia was the biggest threat in the world.

According to Democrats, Hillary Clinton was a lock to win the presidency in 2016. Hillary was the chosen one. Hillary was the most qualified candidate ever. She had it all- money, fame, experience; no chance she would lose to a racist like Donald Trump. The thought of a candidate like Hillary Clinton losing to someone like Donald Trump was preposterous. Except she did. There had to be a legitimate reason why.

The only explanation Democrats could come up with was the election was rigged and therefore it was illegitimate. That's right, it was rigged and you guessed it- Russia was the one who rigged it. Day in and day out all you heard on cable news was, RUSSIA. It was everywhere. CNN and MSNBC flooded the airwaves with "Russia experts", all of them, not knowing what the hell they were talking about, bloviating about Russian interference. Not a single one of them could actually point to one instance where a single vote was changed. They just repeated the Democrat talking points sent down for the day.

On May 9th, 2017 President Trump fired FBI director, Jim Comey, rightfully so. The firing was completely within the powers granted to President Trump and totally justified. This angered the entire Democratic Party. Keep in mind, the same people who were angered by this were the same people who called for Comey's firing in 2016 when he made his public statements regarding Hillary Clinton. Democrats did not care about Jim Comey, they disliked Donald Trump and anything he did. So, fire someone six months after we call for his firing and you are a traitor. Make sense yet? To Democrats, it made perfect sense.

The firing of Jim Comey was the beginning of the biggest political witch hunt in the history of the United States. It began something the Democrats had been dreaming of since election night, 2016. Eight days after Comey was fired on May 17, 2017 Deputy Attorney General Rod Rosenstein appointed former FBI Director Robert Mueller as special counsel to investigate the 2016 election and any Russian interference.

This was like Christmas morning to the mouth breathers on CNN. This was the end for President Trump. Robert Mueller was a man of integrity, they told us. He would get to the bottom of it, they said. As they always do, they brought in "experts" who would tell their small audience that "Mueller has the goods on Donald Trump". As a result of this "President Trump would soon be impeached". Of course like everything else, they were lying. They were disingenuous and partisan. Truth is, they were hoping this would be true, but had no evidence. They fanned the flames by lying to their audience.

61

This went on for 2 years. On and on every day, the "smart people" on cable news would lie to their viewers. The day finally came for Robert Mueller to explain his findings. May 29th, 2019 was a Christmas morning, your birthday, and anniversary all wrapped in one. Democrats were so excited to hear what Mueller had to say. This was the end, big orange is going down. Mueller was going to show the world that Hillary would have won, if Donald Trump did not collude with Vladimir Putin.

Every liberal from Bangor, Maine, to San Diego, California, tuned in Wednesday to see what their hero, Robert Mueller would say. They wanted to see what evidence he would put forth that would bring the most powerful man in the world down. There is a saying: "never meet your hero". That could not be truer here.

Following a short press conference, Mueller did confirm Russia tried to interfere in the 2016 election. However, he concluded there was no collusion between President Trump and the Kremlin. In fact, Mueller conceded that Russia was not trying to help either candidate, rather they were trying to disrupt our election. Robert Mueller did not say the one thing liberals were wanting-GUILTY!

It did not take long for the liberals to turn on Bob Mueller. The onetime savior of America, now could not be trusted. Many of the same "experts" who claimed their "sources" had all sorts of information that was damning, were now was telling us that Bob Mueller's finding were questionable. From the beginning, we were told, Mueller has the integrity of a saint, but now he can't be trusted. Hmm, I wonder why? Perhaps, CNN viewers didn't want the truth. Perhaps, they wanted to hear, what they wanted to hear.

The Mueller investigation wasted millions of tax dollars, divided our country even further, and for what? To tell us what we already knew: Russia is not an ally of the United States. You would think that following the millions of wasted tax dollars and the humiliation of spending 2 years being completely wrong, Democrats would give up the impeachment dream. Not so! They must impeach him because like a few Democrats have said "we must impeach him or he will win in 2020". Got that? If we don't take him out and undo a free and fair election, the voters will elect him again. What a disgrace that many Democrats want to overthrow an election simply because they know they can't win. Given that, it would not take long before they came up with another reason to impeach President Trump.

The list of different reasons Democrats called for impeachment is painfully long. None of them made sense, but logic is something Democrats were short of when it comes to impeaching President Trump. Their pure hatred of him, overruled logic. It would only take 2 weeks after President Trump was sworn into office, before Democrats in the House would call for impeachment. Joaquin Castro of Texas called for President Trump to be removed from office. Why? Not because of a high crime or treason as required by the Constitution. No, Mr. Castro wanted President Trump impeached because Mr. Trump wanted to protect American citizens by enacting a travel ban on countries who did not have proper vetting processes in place. If that that sounds dumb, consider Maxine Watters of California. Auntie Maxine, less than a week later, called for President Trump to be impeached because "we have to" and because Trump was "creating chaos and division".[26] There you have it folks, a sitting Congresswoman wants to impeach a duly elected president because he's mean. No, the real "crime" that took place was Donald Trump beat Hillary Clinton. That's the entire reason "he should be impeached". He beat Hillary, and for that he should be punished.

In the beginning, it was only the fringe who were calling for President Trump's impeachment. The howls were becoming more frequent and louder with every passing day. But as long as the Republicans controlled the House, the cries would be ignored.

Midterm elections usually favor the party not in the White House. 2018 would be no different, as Republicans lost 41 seats in the House returning the gavel to Nancy Pelosi. Nancy Pelosi has been in politics for many years and is a shrewd politician. Having been around the block she knew how to use the power that comes with being Speaker of the House. There is no chance that she would let a freshman Congresswoman from New York bully her around, or at least it would seem like it.

Alexandria Ocasio-Cortez (AOC) was elected to the House of Representatives in the midterm election of 2018. Representing New York's 14th district, she was a very outspoken critic of Donald Trump. Full of energy, the young Congresswoman set her sights on impeachment now that the Democrats were in control the House. The borderline socialist was very zealous. Thanks to her socialist ideas of giving everything away for free and being very charismatic, she quickly built up a large and vocal following. Actors, musicians, college kids, even other politicians looked to AOC for policy direction. As AOC began regularly calling for Donald Trump's impeachment, many others quickly lined up to follow her lead.

The notoriety the young Congresswoman was receiving angered House Speaker Nancy Pelosi. Speaker Pelosi despised Donald Trump, but knowing full well impeachment was going nowhere, never wanted to actually impeach President Trump. Speaker Pelosi only wanted to talk about impeachment. She wanted her "safe" members, members in solidly Democrat districts, to call for impeachment. While the "vulnerable" members, those in moderate districts, never had to actually vote to impeach President Trump. Nancy knew full well she would be reelected so she would take the heat for not bringing impeachment up for a vote, thus protecting the members in the House who were in moderate districts.

The Democrats spent two years blaming Hillary's lose in 2016 on Russia. They spent two years trying to convince America that the only reason President Trump won was he colluded with Vladimir Putin, only to have that argument destroyed by Robert Mueller. It would seem like they would give up the idea of impeachment. At least it would seem. It's not like they don't want to impeach him, they just have to find a reason. If Russia didn't bring President Trump down, perhaps a smaller Slavic speaking country might.

Chapter 12

Impeachment 2.0

The Democrats have already figured out they could not beat President Trump in 2020. The Democrats saw from the first year President Trump was in office that he was truly Making America Great Again. They knew no policy they run on would convince Americans to kick someone out of the White House that had presided over a booming economy, record unemployment, growing wages, and consumer confidence at an all-time high. Given all of that, they knew impeachment was the only thing that would give them a punchers chance. They tried several tactics for impeachment- Emoluments Clause, spreading hate, and Russia; all failed big! Alas, they may have their smoking gun..

Back in April of 2014, then Vice-President, Joe Biden was the point man for Russia's neighbor to the east, Ukraine. Joe Biden was in charge of building relations with Ukraine, especially taking interest in oil and natural gas. Ukraine had an abundance of both oil and natural gas. President Obama wanted to tap into the resources Ukraine had to offer. President Obama tasked Joe Biden with securing a deal suitable for both sides.

Joe Biden has a son named Hunter Biden. Hunter Biden graduated from Georgetown and later got his law degree from Yale. A lawyer by trade, who had zero experience in oil and gas. He also had no knowledge of how the oil and gas industry worked yet was appointed as a board member on a Ukrainian oil and gas company named Burisma Holdings. While he served on the board he was highly compensated, making a whopping $50k per month. How is it that a person with no experience can land that lucrative of a job? You know the answer. Having the same last name as the sitting Vice President helps.

Burisma Holdings, was owned by a Ukrainian oligarch named, Mykola Zlochevsky. Ukraine had always been known for corruption. In 2015, Victor Shokin became the prosecutor in charge of cleaning up the corruption Zlochevsky had been being investigated for (money laundering) since 2012. Shokin picked up the investigation when he was appointed prosecutor in 2015. This investigation could certainly jeopardize American relations with the oil and gas company as well as jeopardize Hunter Biden's lucrative job. Such a thing could not happen if you are Joe Biden, in charge of securing an oil and gas deal for America, and have a son sitting on the board of the very company being investigated.

In December 2015, Vice President Joe Biden made a trip to Kiev. While at a meeting, Biden warned the Ukraine President that if Victor Shokin was not fired America would withhold the $1 billion in loan guarantee. Joe Biden later joked about it saying

"I said, I'm telling you, you're not getting the billion dollars. I said, you're not getting the billion. I'm going to be leaving here in, I think it was about six hours. I looked at them and said: I'm leaving in six hours. If the prosecutor is not fired, you're not getting the money. Well, son of a bitch. He got fired. And they put in place someone who was solid at the time"[27]

By solid, of course he meant corrupt and would not investigate a matter that could jeopardize a deal he wanted. So, it's easy to see the massive corruption in Ukraine. Fast-forward to 2019 and the Democrats control the House and desperately want to impeach President Trump, but without any new revelations, Nancy Pelosi will not allow it.

One of a Presidents jobs is to communicate with the leaders of other countries. On July 25, 2019, President Trump had a phone conversation with the newly elected President of Ukraine, Volodymyr Zelensky. Throughout the 30 minute conversation the two presidents talked about various topics. Mostly it was a congratulatory phone call, but the topic of corruption in the Ukraine came up. President Zelensky promised he was going to fix the huge problem they had. President Trump asked what happened with the prosecutor who was looking into Burisma getting fired. President Zelensky said he would look into why the investigation was shut down. The conversation went on for a little bit longer, mostly small talk, trying to build a relationship.

Phone conversations between foreign leaders are not recorded, rather relying on a group of transcribers who listen in on the conversations and write the conversations down. Typically five or so people listen in and take notes. The transcribers then get together, compare notes, and finally a completed draft is composed.

In the days following President Trump's phone call with the Ukrainian President, an unknown, unnamed whistleblower reported to Adam Schiff of California that he had been informed by someone that President Trump was using his power as president to solicit interference from a foreign country in the 2020 election. The whistleblower alleged that on the July 25th phone call between President Trump and President Zelensky, President Trump asked that Joe Biden and Hunter Biden be investigated. This was it according to Adam Schiff. This was the smoking gun that he, and all the other Democrats had been wishing for since November 8, 2016.

The heart of the matter had to do with foreign aid that the United States was set to deliver to Ukraine. The whistleblower alleged that President Trump tied the foreign aid to an investigation into Joe Biden, who was running for president in 2020. In the Democrats eyes, they saw this as President Trump using his power in the White House to investigate a political opponent and bribing Ukraine to investigate the matter if they wanted the money. Like so many other things regarding Russia or impeachment, it was all a lie.

Adam Schiff likes to be in front of cameras and hear himself talk so he made the most of this opportunity. He spoke to anyone who would listen, claiming he had evidence that would bring President Trump down. This excited the media as they wanted to bring Trump down as well. For days this went on, and Adam Schiff's lies continued to grow. He actually made up a bogus story about what the phone call included. Making outrageous claims of mafia style threats and obvious quid pro quos. He was finally called out on the bogus claims. Schiff claimed he was parodying the conversation. The truth is, Adam Schiff was outright lying and hoping the transcript would not get released. And mostly counting on his uninformed followers believing every word he said. Schiff continued beating the impeachment drum and impeachment began to build steam in the Democrat controlled House.

Once AOC got involved, impeachment was a certainty. AOC being very vocal ginned up the base even more. This put enormous pressure on Nancy Pelosi, who it seems did not want to impeach. So without a shred of evidence on September 24th Nancy Pelosi announced the House would begin an impeachment inquiry.

The time had come for Democrats to make their case for impeachment. Hour upon hour, the Democrats rolled out witness after witness who couldn't tell us one law that was broken. Couldn't tell us one crime that had been committed, only relying on stories of how Donald Trump hurt their feelings or how Donald Trump fired some ambassador that really liked their job. The American people could see this process for what it was- a sham! The public quickly lost interest in impeachment even began to turn on the Democrats as their poll numbers dropped rapidly. This did not matter if you were a Democrat, you controlled the House and you hated Donald Trump, impeachment was happening.

Following the one-sided investigation of impeachment, Donald John Trump was officially impeached on December 18th, 2019, becoming the 3rd president in the history of our country to be impeached. Off to the Senate went the articles of impeachment, where a certain acquittal awaited.**

Millions of tax dollars wasted, lies told to the public, and dividing our country even further is another example of how the Democrats do not care about Americans. Very many people were angered by this process the Democrats put forth. Americans may forgive them in the end, but voting them back in power will be a long shot.

** This section was written prior to Trump's acquittal, which officially occured on February 5, 2020.

Chapter 13

Democrat Split

Politically correct, cancel-culture, being woke, seeking virtue signaling, and trying to be the most progressive person in America are some of the earmarks of the Democratic Party in 2020. While these ideas may make the rich, white liberals in Manhattan feel good about themselves, they do little good for our great nation. The modern Democrat Party is at war. It is at war with itself and it is at war with modern America. The war within the party stems from a division of a more moderate wing of the party and a more progressive wing.

This war started in 2016, with the emergence of Bernie Sanders. Prior to Sanders running for president in 2016, Bernie was a Socialist Senator from Vermont. Being from a small state, outside of Washington D.C. Bernie was not well known. That all changed when he decided to run for president in 2016. His socialist ideas really resonated with the voters, mostly the youth of America. Even though many voters wanted Bernie Sanders to win the nomination, the DNC was never going to allow that. They rigged the system in favor of Hillary Clinton so she would become the first woman to run for president. Very little was said by Bernie, but his supporters were pissed off. Many of them vowed not to vote for Hillary and even some voted against her, to stick it to the establishment.

The fact that Bernie had so many loyal followers, and due to the fact that Hillary failed to win the general election, many other politicians have begun to embrace the socialist ideas Bernie supports. Since the 2016 many in the party have made Bernie's idea their own ideas; even expanding on them. This scares the leaders at the DNC, who only care about power and want to win the White House. They understand that America is not a socialist country, nor will voters ever embrace the ideas the kooks on the far left propose. So now that Bernie is running again in 2020, the establishment will do it to Bernie again. They will do everything in their power to stop Bernie at all cost.

They fear Bernie more than any other candidate. Yes, they all embrace these dumb ideas; but Bernie is the only one who is sincere. Everything Bernie says he will do, he will do. Take money out of politics, Bernie will try. Break up big tech companies, Bernie will do it. Raise taxes to 80%, Bernie will certainly try. These ideas scare the establishment because it means their money and power will evaporate, and that can't happen.

The war with Middle America is more complex. The war started many years ago and has continued through the years, only getting fiercer with the development of social media. Being politically correct is now a religion to the left. Policies, behavior, and speech MUST BE deemed politically correct by the thought police. If not, they will attack you on Twitter and try to take everything they can from you. Say something they do not like and the thought police will instruct the keyboard warriors on Twitter to boycott a business, attack someone's family, whatever they can do to feel virtuous.

This nonsense started in Academia and quickly spread to modern society. No longer is someone allowed to have a belief that is not acceptable to the left. Words or phrases that used to be acceptable can now be considered hate speech, simply because a liberal professor deems it so.

The Democratic Party is obsessed with power and control. Preaching political correctness works perfectly for the modern left. It allows Democrats to control your thoughts and speech by forming a mob and attacking someone with whom they disagree. Most people don't want to be attacked so they just conform, which is what Democrats seek the most- CONFORMITY.

Studies show, a majority of Americans believe America is too politically correct. That doesn't matter to the Democrats, they adhere to it and expect you to as well. This is one of the reasons the Democrats hate President Trump so much. He is unapologetic about not being politically correct. For that they loathe him. They loathe you too, by the way.

The left uses political correctness as a tool to attack anyone they disagree with. Best example is Chick-Fil-A.

Chick-Fil-A has been serving delicious chicken sandwiches and waffle fries to mall goers in America for many years. Founded by the Cathy family, the Chick-Fil-A brand is known for supporting traditional marriage. S. Truett Cathy was a devout Christian man. That Christianity still stands in the company values today. Closed on Sundays, supporting groups that uphold their values is a few examples. The company believed in the traditional marriage of a man and woman. This was unacceptable to the left. Throughout the years Chick-Fil-A has been attacked for their beliefs by every group you could imagine.

It all began in 2012, when COO Dan Cathy made a public statement saying he disagreed with same-sex marriage. This started a firestorm. Politicians, LGBT groups, the ACLU, actors and musicians directed their minions on social media to boycott Chick-Fil-A. The entire company must be shut down because the COO has a different belief than us. Keep in mind, no employee was fired for supporting same-sex marriage, nobody was demoted, and nobody was harmed. That was of little consequence to the left. Chick-Fil-A must go and oh by the way, let this be an example to the rest of you. Disagree with our policies and we will come after you.

Modern America rejects what's known as "cancel-culture". Say or do something liberals oppose and they will work to shut down your way of life. Cancel-Culture is driven by the P.C. crowd. Television shows, movies, singers, actors, comedians, anyone who makes a living performing for people are in the crosshairs. They all fear it because they know if they do or say anything controversial, the mob will come after them. This has caused the decline of T.V. shows, movies, and comedy. Stand-up comedians is a dying trade. Nobody wants to be branded a racist or a sexist or whatever the mob will attack you with so people just go along and are politically correct.

Traditionally comedians would push the line. Comedians

typically had something to say to make us laugh and really didn't care who got offended. If they said something controversial, who cares? That's kind of the idea and it was a joke, so get over it. That's no longer the case. The thought police and the keyboard warriors on Twitter are far too strong now. So many comedians found other lines of work or go broke because they have to talk about boring stuff the thought police will accept.

"You can never be woke enough for the woke crowd". This is such a true statement by Fox News' Tucker Carlson. The left is obsessed with being woke. They use identity politics to divide people into groups, and then assign certain things that is acceptable to say or do to these groups. The woke crowd often attacks each other because they want to be perceived as more woke than anyone else. Because they want to seem more woke, anytime someone comes up with a dumb idea, another politician comes along and comes up with a dumber idea to try and one up the other person. Then the majority of the country is sitting back watching these buffoons try to outdo each other, knowing they will not vote for either.

Chapter 14

Future Republicans

This book was written as a reminder to the post Donald Trump Republican Party. President Trump has shown you the way to win. Want to stay in the White House forever? Follow the play book laid out by President Trump and it can happen.

1. Believe in something and be proud of what you believe in. You can't be halfhearted on your beliefs and expect people to vote for you. Not one time in 2016 did Donald Trump waiver from the idea that we need a wall. Even though he was attacked by the media for it, he stood firm. Too often before Donald Trump, RINO's would have a conservative belief when talking to the conservative crowd, then moderate it when they spoke to a moderate crowd, and all too often, abandon conservative beliefs all together when they were confronted by Democrats. This will not work. We are not stupid. We can see right through your tactics. We will abandon you on Election Day, if you fold when the going gets tough.

2. Be prepared to fight. Things will not be easy. You will be attacked for having conservative beliefs. Fight back. We have your back. Even when the media tells you, the majority is against you, they are lying. We are the majority, but by nature

we are quiet. Don't be discouraged when the polls show you losing, the polls don't reflect our opinions. Anyone can make a poll say what they want it to say. The only poll that matters is in November.

3. Actually care about America. Put forth policies that actually help Americans. Don't worry about your donors, they only have one vote just like us. Do what your voters want. It goes a long way in getting someone to actually vote for you. We can tell if you are disingenuous and we can tell if you are a phony just wanting a vote.

4. Above all else, put America first and we will turn out for you. Become a globalist and we will stay home in November.

5. Donald Trump is Making America Great Again, it will be up to you to keep America great.

Conclusion

This book was written to justify my belief that thanks to an effective leader like Donald Trump in the White House, we will never see another Democrat in office. I hope you see how his policies will help strengthen America all while destroying the Democrat Party. Things can certainly change. The future Republican Party might not learn a lesson from Donald Trump, but I hope they will. The Democrats can get tired of losing and become more moderate, but I doubt that will happen.

References

1. Jeff Gerth, "Clintons joining S&L. Operator in an Ozark Real-Estate Venture New York Times 3-8-92
2. Johnathan Broder and Murry Waas "The road to Hale" Salon.com 3-17-98
3. Murray Waas. "The story Starr did not want to hear" Salon.com 8-17-98
4. Nicholas Confessore & Karen Yourish, Measuring Donald Trump's Mammoth Advantage in Free Media The New York Times 3-16-2016
5. Hillary Clinton says half of Trump's supporters are in a "basket of deplorables" CBS News 9-10-16
6. BLS.gov March 2017 12-13-17
7. BLS.gov
8. Countryecomomy.com
9. Countryecomomy.com
10. Rasmussenreports.com Trump's First Year Accomplishments Compiled In Shockingly Long List By Richard Baris
11. Arrest for illegal crossings hit a 46 year low NPR John Burnett 12-5-17
12. Realclearpolitics.com Trump's Top 10 achievements of 2018 Steve Cortes

13. Realclearpolitics.com Trump's Top 10 achievements of 2019 Steve Cortes
14. Realclearpolitics.com Trump's Top 10 achievements of 2019 Steve Cortes
15. City and town population taken 2-10-18
16. Ballotpedia.org December 3, 2015 Charles Aull
17. Cincinatti.com Jessie Balnert and Jackie Borchard 1-9-20 Cincinnati Enquire
18. Clevland.com 8-16-19
19. Citizen.org Pennsylvania: Lost jobs, rising deficit and stagnant wages under NAFTA
20. Citizen.org Pennsylvania: Lost jobs, rising deficit and stagnant wages under NAFTA
21. Citizen.org Wisconsin job loss during NAFTA
22. Epi.org NAFTA'S impact on US workers 12-9-13 Jeff Faux
23. Epi.org NAFTA's impact on US workers 12-9-13 Jeff Faux
24. Epi.org NAFTA's impact on US workers 12-9-13 Jeff Faux
25. Epi.org NAFTA's impact on US workers 12-9-13 Jeff Faux
26. Thefederalist.com 9-26-19 Tristan Justice 86 Things the Democrats have cited as a reason to impeach Trump
27. Realclearpolitics.com Flashback, 2018: Joe Biden brags at CFR meeting about withholding aid to Ukraine to force firing of prosecutor

www.ingramcontent.com/pod-product-compliance
Lightning Source LLC
Chambersburg PA
CBHW021453210526
45463CB00002B/764